Big Meg Can Help

by Noah Williams
illustrated by Daniel Renner

Decodable 21

McGraw Hill Education

Bothell, WA • Chicago, IL • Columbus, OH • New York, NY

MHEonline.com

Send all inquiries to:
McGraw-Hill Education
8787 Orion Place
Columbus, OH 43240

ISBN: 978-0-02-136258-5
MHID: 0-02-136258-0

Printed in China

9 10 11 12 13 DSS 28 27 26 25 24

When a cab has a flat, get help!

Big Meg can help.

When a van has no gas, get help!

Big Meg is glad to help.

When a bus has a drip, get help!

Big Meg can help.
Big Meg likes to help a lot.